COOK'S COLLECTION

SMOOTHIES & JUICES

Fuss-free and tasty recipe ideas for the modern cook

CONTENTS

INTRODUCTION

Eat your Greens! The words we hated when we were growing up because a pile of overcooked cabbage on your plate was never very exciting or enticing. Today we're spoilt for choice, and the vegetables on display in supermarkets, farmer's markets and allotments look more like sinful sweets than healthy vegetables! But even with the vast choice of fruit and veggies, it can be hard to include them in our diet all the time.

Well, help is at hand. With over 100 exciting recipes for smoothies and juices this book offers the perfect solution. They're quick and easy to make, will show you how to cram at least the requisite five-a-day into your diet – and the whole family will love them!

So, what's the difference between smoothies and juices? Smoothies are blended whole ingredients, which means that you slowly consume all the fibre, vitamins and minerals from the fruit or vegetables. Other ingredients such as milk, yogurt, herbs, seeds or nuts are added to make an easily digested, filling drink that can replace a meal – a great way to start the day, especially if you want to encourage children to eat healthily. Juices are made by squeezing the liquid from fruit and vegetables, leaving much of the fibre behind. The nutrients in the juice are absorbed by the body almost immediately. It's a great way to take on board more vegetables as their flavours can be easily disguised by other ingredients.

To get you going you will need to find the right machine for the job. There are plenty of them to choose from. For smoothies you'll need a goblet blender with a lid or a hand-held blender that fits into a jug. They can be inexpensive, but you should go for the model with the most powerful motor. Check that the model you've chosen will do the job you want it to.

For juices an electric citrus press is the basic machine, but this will only juice citrus fruits. Juice extractors or juicers are heavy-duty pieces of equipment and ideally you should buy the most sophisticated model you can afford. However, before you buy, decide how often you plan to use it. Think about whether you have enough space on a work surface, as some juicers are heavy to take in and out of a cupboard. If you plan to make large quantities of juice at a time, a model that extrudes the pulp into a separate compartment is worth considering as it will prevent you having to empty out the pulp mid-way. Once you have a clearer idea of your juicing requirements you will need to decide whether you need a masticating juicer or a centrifugal juicer.

Masticating or cold-pressed juicers gently crush the fruit and vegetables at a slow speed before forcing the juice through a wire sieve. They produce larger quantities of juice that retains more nutrients and can be refrigerated in an airtight container for up to 48 hours. Centrifugal juicers are smaller and lighter but can be noisy. The ingredients are fed through a tube and finely chopped before being spun fast so the pulp and juice are separated. However, during this process the juice is heated slightly and it also takes in oxygen, so it should be consumed immediately for maximum benefit.

Once you've decided on your equipment you'll need to choose a recipe, and here the choice is endless. In this book you'll find recipes for every need – Energy, Detox, Rehydrate, Glow or Soothe – with delicious names such as Peach Energizer, Mixed Berry Smoothie, Minted Melon Drink and Cucumber Soother. It's great to start with familiar ingredients if juicing is a new concept for you and the family. There may also be some juices that, at first glance, don't sound promising and might, like Parsley Purifier or Fennel Flush, be an acquired taste, but once you start to experiment and appreciate how they affect your well-being, you'll be intrigued by the combinations – what might have seemed impossible at the start may quite easily become a firm favourite.

Smoothies are extremely versatile, with endless possibilities, and you can use fresh, frozen, canned or dried fruit and vegetables blended with yogurt, milk or dairy-free alternatives. With the addition of herbs such as mint, parsley and lemon balm along with various nuts and seeds you'll be amazed at the variety, combinations and flavours that can be achieved using the recipes in this book. Juices require a little more thought, however. Stick to raw fruit and vegetables in season and choose those in peak condition to get the full range of nutrients. Wherever possible choose organic varieties. If using citrus fruits check that the rinds have not been waxed, or peel the fruit before juicing. Start on the simple recipes with just a few familiar ingredients before embarking on those requiring special, more unusual ones.

If this is your first time making your own smoothies and juices here are some tips for success. Read the manufacturer's instructions. Not all machines are the same and some may have unfamiliar features. Prepare fresh ingredients just before embarking on the recipe and keep the skins intact for maximum benefit. Make sure the pieces are evenly sized – soft ingredients such as berries and bananas can be larger but hard items such as carrots need to be cut small. Always combine liquids with solids before blending. And remember, it's always best to drink freshly prepared smoothies and juices as soon as possible for maximum benefit.

Variety is the spice of life and by eating a varied diet we can absorb the vitamins, minerals, enzymes and antioxidants we need for peak performance and to keep us healthy. Juices and smoothies are a great way to take on board more vegetables and fruits in exciting combinations and the family will love them. With the recipes in this book, you'll never run out of ideas.

CUPS

CHAPTER ONE

ENERGY

CRIMSON VITALITY

SERVES: *4* | **PREP:** *10–15 mins* | **COOK:** *No cooking*

INGREDIENTS

1 beetroot, halved
115 g/4 oz cranberries
1-cm/½-inch piece fresh ginger, peeled
2 apples, quartered
crushed ice (optional)
chilled water, to taste

1. Feed the beetroot halves through a juicer, then feed the cranberries, ginger and apples through the juicer.

2. Put a small handful of crushed ice, if using, into four tall glasses and divide the juice between them.

3. Top up the glasses with some chilled water to taste and serve the juice immediately.

BLUEBERRY BLAST

SERVES: *1* | **PREP:** *10–15 mins* | **COOK:** *No cooking*

INGREDIENTS

1 pear, halved
115 g/4 oz blueberries
175 g/6 oz natural yogurt
20 g/¾ oz wheat germ
175 ml/6 fl oz chilled water
crushed ice (optional)

1. Feed the pear halves through a juicer, then pour the juice into a blender or food processor.

2. Add the blueberries, yogurt, wheat germ and chilled water to the blender and blend until smooth.

3. Add a small handful of crushed ice, if using, and blend again until smooth. Pour into a glass and serve immediately.

RED PEPPER REVIVER

SERVES: *1* | **PREP:** *10–15 mins* | **COOK:** *No cooking*

INGREDIENTS

2 carrots, halved
2 tomatoes, halved
1 large red pepper, deseeded and halved
2 tsp lemon juice
pinch of pepper, plus extra to garnish (optional)
4–6 strips of shredded carrot, to garnish

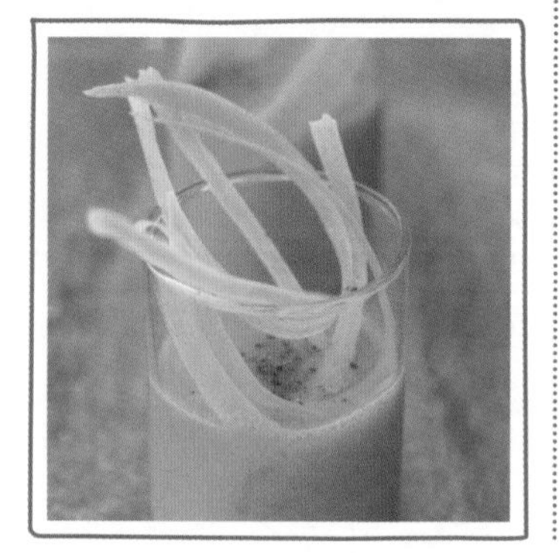

1. Feed the carrot halves through a juicer, followed by the tomato and red pepper halves.

2. Add the lemon juice and a pinch of pepper to the juice and stir well to combine.

3. Pour the juice into a tall glass, garnish with the strips of shredded carrot and pepper, if using, and serve immediately.

BLUEBERRY THRILL

SERVES: *2* | **PREP:** *10 mins* | **COOK:** *No cooking*

INGREDIENTS

100 g/3½ oz Greek-style natural yogurt
100 ml/3½ fl oz water
125 g/4½ oz frozen blueberries
2 whole frozen blueberries, to decorate

1. Put the yogurt into a blender with the water and the frozen blueberries and blend until smooth.

2. Pour the smoothie into two glasses, top each one with a whole frozen blueberry and serve immediately.

TROPICAL ENERGIZER

SERVES: *1* | **PREP:** *15–20 mins* | **COOK:** *No cooking*

INGREDIENTS

1 banana, peeled and roughly chopped
½ papaya, peeled, deseeded and roughly chopped
½ mango, stoned, peeled and roughly chopped
juice of 1 lime
2-cm/¾-inch piece fresh ginger, peeled and finely grated
2 tsp hemp oil
125 ml/4 fl oz unsweetened rice, almond or soya milk
crushed ice

1. Put the chopped banana, papaya and mango into a blender and blend until smooth.

2. Add the lime juice, ginger, hemp oil and rice milk to the blender with a small handful of crushed ice and blend again.

3. Pour the juice into a tall glass and serve immediately with a straw.

ALMOND BUTTER & RASPBERRY BLISS

SERVES: *2* | **PREP:** *10 mins* | **COOK:** *No cooking*

INGREDIENTS

1 banana, peeled and roughly chopped
200 g/7 oz raspberries
400 ml/14 fl oz unsweetened almond milk
40 g/1½ oz almond butter
4 tsp stevia granules
2 tsp vanilla extract
ice cubes

1. Put the chopped banana into a blender with the raspberries, then add the almond milk, almond butter and stevia granules.

2. Add the vanilla extract and top up with ice cubes, then blend until smooth and combined.

3. Pour the smoothie into two glasses and serve immediately with straws, or chill in the refrigerator overnight.

1

2

2

GINGER PEP-UP

SERVES: *1* | **PREP:** *10 mins* | **COOK:** *No cooking*

INGREDIENTS

2 pears, halved
juice of 4 oranges
4 cubes crystallized ginger

1. Feed the pears halves through a juicer, then pour the pear juice into a blender.

2. Add the orange juice and the crystallized ginger to the blender and whizz until smooth.

3. Pour the juice into a glass and serve immediately.

BERRY KICK-START

SERVES: *1* | **PREP:** *10–15 mins* | **COOK:** *No cooking*

INGREDIENTS

175 g/6 oz blueberries
115 g/4 oz cranberries
150 g/5½ oz natural yogurt
2 tsp clear honey
4 tbsp chilled water

1. Put the blueberries and cranberries into a blender and blend until they have broken down.

2. Add the yogurt, honey and chilled water to the blender and blend again until smooth.

3. Pour the juice into a glass and serve immediately.

RAW CACAO MILKSHAKE

SERVES: *4* | **PREP:** *10 mins* | **COOK:** *No cooking*

INGREDIENTS

400 ml/14 fl oz almond milk
85 g/3 oz dried dates
85 g/3 oz cashew nuts
2 tbsp raw cacao powder
1 tsp ground cinnamon
ice cubes
1 tbsp orange zest, to decorate

1. Place the almond milk in a blender and add the dates, nuts, cacao powder and cinnamon.

2. Add a handful of ice cubes to the blender, then blend thoroughly until the mixture has a thick pouring consistency.

3. Pour the milkshake into four chilled glasses, decorate with the orange zest and serve immediately.

2

2

3

GINGER ENERGIZER

SERVES: *1* | **PREP:** *15 mins* | **COOK:** *No cooking*

INGREDIENTS

2 carrots, halved
4 tomatoes, roughly chopped
1 tbsp lemon juice
25 g/1 oz fresh flat-leaf parsley
3-cm/1¼-inch piece fresh ginger, peeled and finely grated
crushed ice
125 ml/4 fl oz chilled water

1. Feed the carrot halves through a juicer. Pour the juice into a blender, add the chopped tomatoes and the lemon juice and blend.

2. Add the parsley (reserving a sprig to decorate), ginger and a small handful of crushed ice and blend again until smooth. Add the chilled water and whizz again.

3. Pour the juice into a tall glass, garnish with the parsley sprig and serve immediately.

APPLE & PLUM POWER BOOST

SERVES: *2* | **PREP:** *15 mins* | **COOK:** *15 mins, plus chilling*

INGREDIENTS

1 ripe pear, peeled and quartered
1 apple, peeled and quartered
2 large red or dark plums, halved and stoned
4 ripe damsons, halved and stoned
200 ml/7 fl oz water
slices of apple or pear, to decorate

1. Put the pear and apple quarters into a small saucepan with the plum and damson halves.

2. Add the water, then cover tightly, set over a medium heat and bring slowly to the boil. Remove from the heat and leave to cool, then chill in the refrigerator

3. Put the fruit and water mixture into a food processor or blender and process until smooth.

4. Pour the juice into two glasses, decorate with slices of apple or pear and serve immediately.

POWER GULP

SERVES: *1* | **PREP:** *10–15 mins* | **COOK:** *No cooking*

INGREDIENTS

2 beetroots, halved
25 g/1 oz linseeds
4 plums, quartered and stoned
150 g/5½ oz seedless red grapes
225 ml/8 fl oz chilled water
ice cubes, to serve (optional)

1. Feed the beetroot halves through a juicer. Put the linseeds into a blender and whizz until finely ground.

2. Add the beetroot juice, plum quarters, grapes and chilled water to the blender and blend until smooth.

3. Pour the juice into a glass, add some ice cubes, if using, and serve immediately.

AÇAI & BERRY MORNING JAR

SERVES: *1* | **PREP:** *10 mins, plus resting and chilling* | **COOK:** *No cooking*

INGREDIENTS

90 g/3¼ oz strawberries
90 g/3¼ oz raspberries
35 g/1¼ oz blueberries
150 g/5½ oz coconut yogurt
50 ml/2 fl oz coconut milk
½ tsp seeds from 1 vanilla pod
1 tbsp chia seeds
2 tsp honey
1 tsp acai powder
½ tbsp lemon juice
2 tbsp cashew butter
1 tsp hemp seeds
2 fresh mint sprigs

1. Put 70 g/2½ oz of the strawberries, 70 g/2½ oz of the raspberries and 25 g/1 oz of the blueberries into a blender with the coconut yogurt, coconut milk, vanilla seeds, chia seeds, honey, acai powder and lemon juice and blend until smooth.

2. Pour the mixture into a wide-necked jar with a 300–325-ml/10–11 fl-oz capacity. Cover and chill in the refrigerator overnight.

3. The following morning, top the smoothie with the cashew butter and the remaining berries. Add the hemp seeds and mint sprigs and serve immediately.

PEACH ENERGIZER

SERVES: *1* | **PREP:** *15–20 mins* | **COOK:** *No cooking*

INGREDIENTS

1 pink or ruby grapefruit, zest and a little pith removed, halved
1 carrot, halved
1-cm/½-inch piece fresh ginger, peeled
1 large peach, stoned and roughly chopped
1 tbsp light tahini
125 ml/4 fl oz chilled water (optional)
crushed ice

1. Feed the grapefruit halves through a juicer, followed by the carrot halves and the ginger.

2. Pour the juice into a blender, then add the chopped peach, tahini and the chilled water, if using.

3. Add a small handful of crushed ice and blend until smooth, then pour the juice into a tall glass and serve immediately.

VEGETABLE BELLY TREAT

SERVES: *1* | **PREP:** *15–20 mins* | **COOK:** *No cooking*

INGREDIENTS

3 oranges, zest and a little pith removed
1 carrot, halved
2 tomatoes, roughly chopped
125 ml/4 fl oz chilled water
1 small green chilli, halved
2 celery sticks, thickly sliced
2 tsp hemp seed oil

1. Cut 2 of the oranges in half and feed them through a juicer with the carrot halves. Pour the juice into a blender.

2. Roughly chop and deseed the remaining orange, then put it into the blender with the chopped tomatoes and the chilled water and blend until smooth.

3. Add the chilli and the celery sticks and blend again until smooth. Pour the juice into a glass, add the hemp seed oil and stir to combine, then serve immediately.

POWER-BOOSTING BEET

SERVES: *1* | **PREP:** *10–15 mins* | **COOK:** *No cooking*

INGREDIENTS

2 beetroots, halved
2 large carrots, halved
2 celery sticks, halved
5-cm/2-inch piece cucumber
2 red-skinned apples, halved
25 g/1 oz walnut pieces, finely ground
crushed ice (optional)

1. Cut two wafer-thin slices off one of the beetroot halves and reserve to garnish.

2. Feed the beetroot and carrot halves through a juicer, followed by the celery stick halves, the cucumber and the apple halves. Stir in the walnut pieces.

3. Put a small handful of crushed ice, if using, into a glass, then pour the juice over the ice.

4. Thread the reserved beetroot slices through a cocktail stick, lay this on top of the glass and serve immediately.

STRAWBERRY & VANILLA DELIGHT

SERVES: *2* | **PREP:** *10–15 mins* | **COOK:** *No cooking*

INGREDIENTS

200 g/7 oz strawberries
200 g/7 oz plain soya yogurt
100 ml/3½ fl oz chilled soya milk
2 tsp vanilla extract

1. Pick over the strawberries, then hull and halve them and place them in a small bowl.

2. Transfer the strawberry halves to a blender, add the yogurt, milk and vanilla extract and gently blend until thoroughly combined.

3. Pour the smoothie into two tall glasses and serve immediately.

RED PEP-UP

SERVES: *1* | **PREP:** *15 mins* | **COOK:** *No cooking*

INGREDIENTS

2 fennel bulbs with fronds, halved
1 apple, halved
1 small red pepper, halved
1 carrot, halved

1. Remove a few fronds from the fennel and reserve to garnish.

2. Feed the apple halves through a juicer, followed by the fennel and red pepper halves, then the carrot halves.

3. Pour the juice into a glass, garnish with the reserved fennel fronds and serve immediately.

1
2
2

BERRY SUNRISE SMOOTHIE

SERVES: *1* | **PREP:** *10 mins* | **COOK:** *No cooking*

INGREDIENTS

1 banana, peeled and roughly chopped
55 g/2 oz silken tofu, drained and roughly chopped
175 ml/6 fl oz orange juice
200 g/7 oz frozen mixed berries

1. Place the chopped banana, chopped tofu, orange juice and frozen berries in a large bowl or jug.

2. Using a hand-held blender, process on high speed until smooth. Leave the smoothie to settle for a few seconds, then process again until fully blended.

3. Pour the smoothie into a tall glass, lightly stir, then serve immediately with straws.

TROPICAL WATERMELON WONDER

SERVES: *2* | **PREP:** *15 mins* | **COOK:** *No cooking*

INGREDIENTS

1 watermelon wedge, weighing about 600 g/1 lb 5 oz, peeled, deseeded and roughly chopped
2 small bananas, peeled and roughly chopped
225 ml/8 fl oz coconut cream

1. Put the chopped watermelon, chopped bananas and coconut cream into a blender.

2. Process until smooth and combined, then pour the smoothie into two chilled glasses and serve immediately.

CHAPTER TWO

DETOX

PARSLEY PURIFIER

SERVES: *1* | **PREP:** *10–15 mins* | **COOK:** *No cooking*

INGREDIENTS

115 g/4 oz sugar snap peas
small handful of fresh flat-leaf parsley
2 fresh rosemary sprigs
1 garlic clove
55 g/2 oz young spinach
½ cucumber
2 celery sticks, halved
1 tsp hemp seed oil
chilled water, to taste
ice cubes, to serve (optional)

1. Feed the peas, parsley (reserving 1 sprig to garnish), rosemary and garlic through a juicer, followed by the spinach, cucumber and celery stick halves.

2. Pour the juice into a tall glass, then add the hemp seed oil and some chilled water to taste and stir to combine.

3. Garnish the glass with the reserved parsley sprig and serve the juice with ice cubes, if using.

BEET AID DETOX

SERVES: *1* | **PREP:** *10 mins* | **COOK:** *No cooking*

INGREDIENTS

1 beetroot, halved
½ lime, zest and pith removed, deseeded and roughly chopped
55 g/2 oz red chard
675 g/1 lb 8 oz watermelon, thickly sliced and peeled
crushed ice (optional)

1. Feed the beetroot halves and the chopped lime through a juicer, followed by the chard and the watermelon slices.

2. Put a small handful of crushed ice, if using, into a tall glass.

3. Pour the juice over the ice and serve immediately with a straw.

BRIGHT EYES

SERVES: *1* | **PREP:** *15 mins, plus cooling* | **COOK:** *No cooking*

INGREDIENTS

100 ml/3½ fl oz boiling water
1 green tea sachet, or 1 tsp green tea
1 carrot, roughly chopped
1 apple, halved
small handful of fresh flat-leaf parsley
1–2 fresh flat-leaf parsley sprigs, to garnish

1. Pour the boiling water onto the green tea and leave to stand for 4 minutes. Strain and leave to cool slightly.

2. Put the chopped carrot, apple halves and parsley into a food processor or blender and process until smooth. Stir the mixture into the green tea.

3. Pour the juice into a glass and serve warm or cold, garnished with parsley sprigs.

RED CABBAGE DIGESTIVE AID

SERVES: *1* | **PREP:** *15 mins* | **COOK:** *No cooking*

INGREDIENTS

150 g/5½ oz red grapes
½ fennel bulb, roughly chopped
¼ head of red cabbage, roughly chopped
3 cardamom pods
chilled water, to taste
crushed ice (optional)

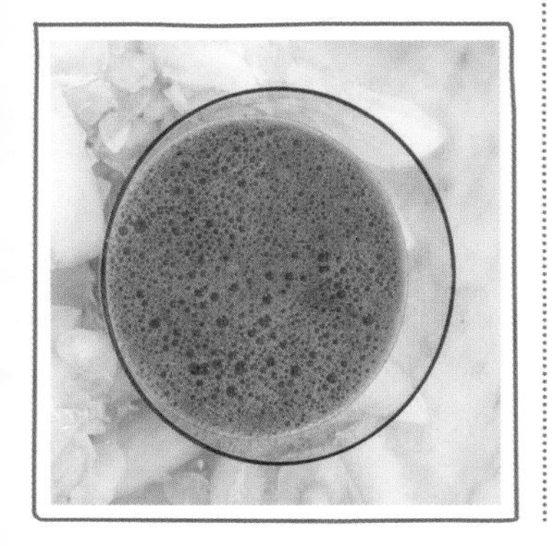

1. Feed the grapes through a juicer, followed by the chopped fennel and the chopped cabbage.

2. Roughly crush the cardamom pods in a mortar with a pestle and discard the pods, then finely crush the black seeds and stir them into the juice. Top up with chilled water to taste.

3. Put a small handful of crushed ice, if using, into a glass, then pour the juice over the ice and serve immediately.

DANDELION SUNRISE

SERVES: *1* | **PREP:** *10–15 mins* | **COOK:** *No cooking*

INGREDIENTS

25 g/1 oz dandelion leaves
55 g/2 oz curly green kale, shredded
200 ml/7 fl oz chilled water
25 g/1 oz cashew nuts
½ tbsp coconut butter
1 tbsp sunflower seeds

1. Put the dandelion leaves into a blender with the shredded kale and chilled water and blend until smooth.

2. Add the cashew nuts, coconut butter and sunflower seeds to the blender and blend until the mixture is smooth and creamy.

3. Pour the smoothie into a glass and serve immediately with a straw.

PINE-NETTLE SMOOTHIE

SERVES: *2* | **PREP:** *15–20 mins* | **COOK:** *No cooking*

INGREDIENTS

NETTLE LAYER

100 g/3½ oz nettle leaves, rinsed and blanched
1 apple, cored and roughly chopped
1 lemon, peeled and roughly chopped
2 stoned dates, quartered
¼ tsp dried ginger
100 ml/3½ fl oz orange juice

PINEAPPLE LAYER

450 g/1 lb fresh pineapple, peeled and cored
100 g/3½ oz soya yogurt
25 g/1 oz rolled oats

1. To make the nettle layer, put the nettle leaves, chopped apple, chopped lemon, date quarters, ginger and orange juice into a blender and blend until smooth. Transfer to a jug and rinse the blender.

2. To make the pineapple layer, chop the pineapple into bite-sized pieces. Place the pieces in the blender, add the yogurt and oats and blend until smooth.

3. Carefully layer the nettle and pineapple mixtures in two large glasses and serve immediately with straws.

1
1
2

GREEN JUMP START

SERVES: *1* | **PREP:** *10 mins* | **COOK:** *No cooking*

INGREDIENTS

55 g/2 oz young spinach
25 g/1 oz watercress
1 courgette, halved
2 apples, halved
1 tsp wheatgrass powder (optional)
crushed ice (optional)

1. Feed the spinach and watercress through a juicer, followed by the courgette and apple halves.

2. Add the wheatgrass powder, if using, and stir well to combine.

3. Put a small handful of crushed ice, if using, into a glass, then pour the juice over the ice and serve immediately.

GREEN GODDESS

SERVES: *1* | **PREP:** *15 mins* | **COOK:** *No cooking*

INGREDIENTS

½ Galia melon, thickly sliced and peeled
85 g/3 oz young spinach
2 large fresh flat-leaf parsley sprigs
3 large fresh mint sprigs
crushed ice (optional)

1. Feed the melon slices through a juicer, followed by the spinach, then the parsley and two of the mint sprigs.

2. Put a small handful of crushed ice, if using, into a glass, then pour the juice over the ice.

3. Garnish the glass with the remaining mint sprig and serve the juice immediately.

BIG APPLE DETOX

SERVES: *1* | **PREP:** *10 mins* | **COOK:** *No cooking*

INGREDIENTS

1 parsnip, halved
5-mm/¼-inch piece fresh ginger, peeled
2 apples, halved
125 ml/4 fl oz chilled water
crushed ice (optional)

1. Feed the parsnip halves and the ginger through a juicer, followed by the apple halves.

2. Top up the parsnip and apple juice with the chilled water.

3. Put a small handful of crushed ice, if using, into a glass, then pour the juice over the ice and serve immediately.

STRESS BUSTER

SERVES: *1* | **PREP:** *15 mins* | **COOK:** *No cooking*

INGREDIENTS

1 ginseng tea bag or 1 tsp ginseng tea
150 ml/5 fl oz boiling water
1 apple, halved
40 g/1½ oz rocket leaves

1. Put the tea bag into a cup, pour over the boiling water and leave to stand for 4 minutes. Strain the tea into a glass.

2. Feed the apple halves through a juicer, followed by the rocket.

3. Stir the apple juice into the tea, mixing well to combine, and serve warm or cold.

AÇAI KNOCK-OUT

SERVES: *1* | **PREP:** *10 mins* | **COOK:** *No cooking*

INGREDIENTS

75 g/2¾ oz spinach
2 tsp açai powder
2 tsp manuka honey
pinch of ground cinnamon
250 ml/9 fl oz almond milk
crushed ice, to serve

1. Place the spinach, açai powder, honey and a pinch of cinnamon in a blender.

2. Pour over the almond milk and blend until the mixture is smooth and creamy.

3. Put a handful of crushed ice into a tall glass, then stir the juice, pour it over the ice and serve immediately.

GREEN TEA PUNCH

SERVES: *1* | **PREP:** *10–15 mins* | **COOK:** *No cooking*

INGREDIENTS

300 ml/10 fl oz green tea
juice of ½ lemon
¼ tsp liquid ginseng
1 tsp pea protein
1 tsp wheatgrass powder
1 tsp maca powder
ice cubes, to serve

1. Put the green tea, lemon juice, ginseng, pea protein, wheatgrass powder and maca powder into a jug and whisk to combine.

2. Alternatively, you could put all the ingredients into a blender and whizz to combine.

3. Put some ice cubes into a glass, then pour over the green tea punch and serve immediately.

MATCHA POWER SMOOTHIE

SERVES: *1* | **PREP:** *10 mins, plus optional chilling* | **COOK:** *No cooking*

INGREDIENTS

25 g/1 oz spinach
1 banana, peeled and chopped
1 small ripe avocado, stoned, flesh scooped from the skin and roughly chopped
2 kiwi fruit, peeled and chopped
125 ml/4 fl oz raw almond milk
½ tbsp raw honey
1 tsp matcha tea powder
½ tsp wheatgrass powder
2 tsp flaked almonds, to decorate
½ tsp maca powder, to decorate

1. Put the spinach, chopped banana, chopped avocado and one of the chopped kiwi fruit into a blender. Add half the almond milk and blend to a purée.

2. Add the honey, matcha tea powder, wheatgrass and the remaining almond milk and blend until smooth.

3. Pour the smoothie into a serving bowl and chill in the refrigerator for 1 hour if you have time.

4. Top the smoothie with the remaining chopped kiwi fruit, decorate with the flaked almonds and maca powder and serve immediately.

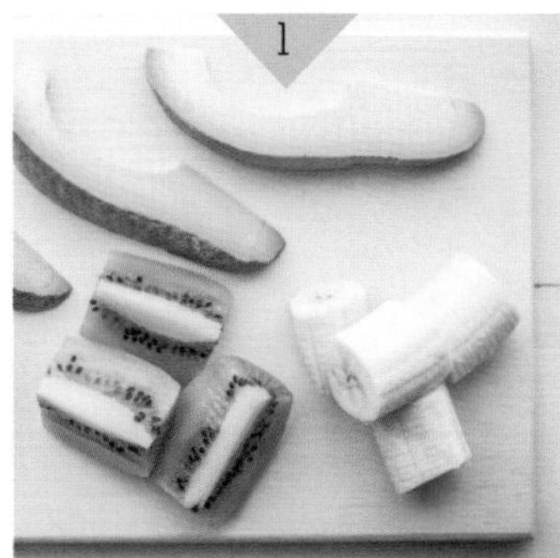
1

1

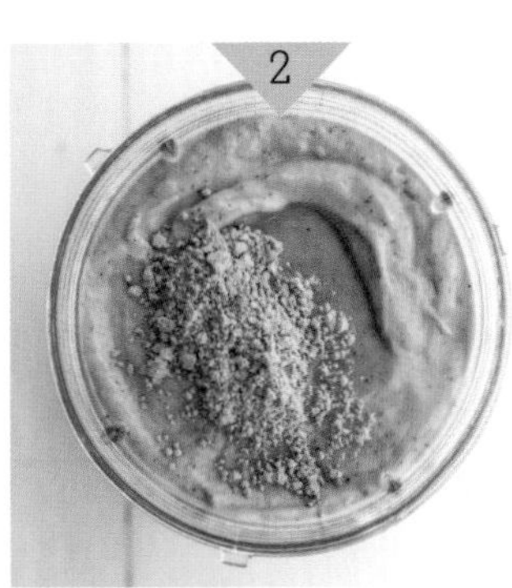
2

GREEN CLEANER

SERVES: *1* | **PREP:** *10 mins* | **COOK:** *No cooking*

INGREDIENTS

1 apple, halved
25 g/1 oz green curly kale
2 kiwi fruit, peeled
2 flat-leaf parsley sprigs
½ avocado, stoned, flesh scooped from the skin and chopped
4 tbsp chilled water
crushed ice

1. Feed the apple halves, kale and kiwi fruit through a juicer.

2. Pour the juice into a blender, add the parsley and avocado pieces and blend until smooth.

3. Add the chilled water and a handful of crushed ice and blend again until smooth.

4. Pour the smoothie into a glass and serve immediately.

NATURE'S REMEDY

SERVES: *1* | **PREP:** *10–15 mins* | **COOK:** *No cooking*

INGREDIENTS

2 carrots, halved
½ small onion, halved
1 garlic clove
1 parsnip, halved
1 orange, zest and a little pith removed, halved
50 ml/2 fl oz chilled water
pinch of ground turmeric
pinch of pepper
crushed ice (optional)

1. Cut a thin slice from one of the carrot halves and reserve to garnish. Feed the carrot halves, onion halves, garlic and the parsnip halves through a juicer, followed by the orange halves.

2. Add the chilled water, ground turmeric and pepper. to the carrot juice and stir well to combine.

3. Put a small handful of crushed ice, if using, into a glass, then pour the juice over the ice, garnish with the reserved carrot slice and serve immediately.

LYCHEE & PINEAPPLE PEP-UP

SERVES: *1* | **PREP:** *20 mins, plus cooling* | **COOK:** *No cooking*

INGREDIENTS

1½ lemon grass stalks
4 tbsp boiling water
6 lychees, peeled and stoned
½ small pineapple, peeled and cut into thick slices
¼ honeydew melon, thickly sliced and peeled
crushed ice (optional)

1. Cut the whole lemon grass stem in half lengthways, then cut it in half crossways. Bruise it with a rolling pin to release its flavour, then put it in a shallow bowl and add the boiling water. Cover and leave to cool completely, then drain, reserving the soaking water.

2. Feed the softened lemon grass, lychees and pineapple slices through a juicer, followed by the melon slices. Mix in the reserved lemon grass soaking water.

3. Put a small handful of crushed ice, if using, into a glass, then pour the juice over the ice and serve immediately with the remaining lemon grass stalk as a stirrer.

FENNEL FLUSH

SERVES: *1* | **PREP:** *10–15 mins* | **COOK:** *No cooking*

INGREDIENTS

100 g/3½ oz spinach
20 g/¾ oz fresh mint
1 large fennel bulb, roughly chopped
1 green apple, halved
1 lime, zest and pith removed, deseeded and roughly chopped
crushed ice, to serve (optional)

1. Feed the spinach, mint, chopped fennel, apple halves and chopped lime through a juicer.

2. Put a handful of crushed ice, if using, into a glass.

3. Stir the juice well, pour it over the ice and serve immediately.

SPINACH AID

SERVES: *1* | **PREP:** *10–15 mins* | **COOK:** *No cooking*

INGREDIENTS

20 g/¾ oz spinach
1 tbsp aloe vera gel
juice of ½ lime
½ tsp spirulina powder
3½ tbsp chilled water

1. Place the spinach, aloe vera gel, lime juice and spirulina powder in a blender.

2. Pour in the chilled water into the blender and blend the mixture until smooth.

3. Pour the juice into a glass and serve immediately.

RAPID RECHARGE

SERVES: *1* | **PREP:** *15 mins* | **COOK:** *No cooking*

INGREDIENTS

1 small courgette, halved
1 celery stick, roughly chopped
40 g/1½ oz baby leaf spinach
40 g/1½ oz alfalfa sprouts
2 apples, peeled and cored
1 tsp alfalfa sprouts, to garnish

1. Put the courgette halves into a blender with the chopped celery. Add the spinach and alfalfa sprouts (reserving a few to garnish), then add the apples.

2. Blend all the ingredients together until smooth, then pour the mixture into a glass.

3. Garnish with the reserved alfalfa sprouts and serve immediately.

CUCUMBER SPRING CLEAN

SERVES: *1* | **PREP:** *10 mins* | **COOK:** *No cooking*

INGREDIENTS

½ head of cos lettuce
2 tomatoes
2-cm/¾-inch piece fresh ginger
1 spring onion
1 celery stick, halved
1 carrot, halved
¼ cucumber
crushed ice (optional)
cucumber slice, to garnish (optional)

1. Feed the lettuce and tomatoes through a juicer, followed by the ginger, spring onion, celery stick halves, carrot halves and cucumber.

2. Put a small handful of crushed ice, if using, into a glass, stir the juice and pour it over the ice,

3. Garnish with the cucumber slice, if using, and serve immediately.

GREEN CRUSH

SERVES: *1* | **PREP:** *10–15 mins* | **COOK:** *No cooking*

INGREDIENTS

100 g/3½ oz kohlrabi or turnip, peeled and chopped
75 g/2¾ oz courgette,chopped
150 ml/5 fl oz chilled water
100 ml/3½ fl oz coconut milk
75 g/2¾ oz avocado, halved, stoned, flesh scooped from the skin and chopped
juice of ½ lime
4 ice cubes
2 lime slices, to garnish

1. Put the chopped kohlrabi and courgette into a blender with the chilled water and coconut milk and blend until smooth and creamy.

2. Add the chopped avocado to the blender with the lime juice and ice cubes, and blend again until smooth.

3. Pour the smoothie into a glass, garnish with the lime slices and serve immediately.

CHAPTER THREE

REHYDRATE

RASPBERRY & WATERMELON CRUSH

SERVES: *1* | **PREP:** *15 mins* | **COOK:** *No cooking*

INGREDIENTS

¼ small watermelon, peeled, roughly chopped and most of the black seeds removed
½ lime, zest and most of the pith removed, deseeded and roughly chopped
100 g/3½ oz raspberries
crushed ice

1. Put the chopped watermelon and the chopped lime into a blender and blend until smooth.

2. Add the raspberries and a small handful of crushed ice and blend again until smooth and combined.

3. Pour the crush into a glass and serve immediately.

GRAPEFRUIT CRUSH

SERVES: *1* | **PREP:** *10–15 mins* | **COOK:** *No cooking*

INGREDIENTS

150 g/5½ oz cucumber, roughly chopped
½ pink grapefruit, zest and a little pith removed, deseeded and roughly chopped
2 kiwi fruit, peeled and roughly chopped
2 celery sticks, roughly chopped
1 tsp maca powder
4 tbsp coconut water
1 pink grapefruit segment, to garnish
crushed ice, to serve (optional)

1. Feed the chopped cucumber, pink grapefruit, kiwi fruit and celery through a juicer.

2. Add the maca powder and coconut water and stir through the juice until combined.

3. Put some crushed ice, if using, into a glass, pour the juice over the ice, garnish with a pink grapefruit segment and serve immediately.

TROPICAL SUNRISE & SHINE

SERVES: *1* | **PREP:** *10–15 mins* | **COOK:** *No cooking*

INGREDIENTS

20 g/¾ oz goji berries
15 g/½ oz chia seeds
½ papaya, peeled, deseeded and roughly chopped
¼ pineapple, peeled and roughly chopped
½ lime, zest and a little pith removed, deseeded and roughly chopped
225 ml/8 fl oz chilled water
crushed ice (optional)

1. Put the goji berries and chia seeds into a blender and whizz until finely ground.

2. Add the chopped papaya, pineapple, lime and the chilled water to the blender and whizz until smooth.

3. Add a small handful of crushed ice, if using, and whizz again until smooth. Pour the juice into a glass and serve immediately.

SUMMER CORN QUENCHER

SERVES: *1* | **PREP:** *15 mins* | **COOK:** *No cooking*

INGREDIENTS

1 fresh corn cob, husks and silks removed
4 fresh coriander sprigs
1 yellow pepper, deseeded and halved
1 apple, halved
crushed ice (optional)

1. Cut the niblets from the corn cob, then feed them through a juicer.

2. Feed the coriander sprigs through the juicer, followed by the yellow pepper and apple halves.

3. Put a small handful of crushed ice, if using, into a glass, then pour the juice over the ice and serve immediately.

COOL AS A CUCUMBER

SERVES: *1* | **PREP:** *10–15 mins* | **COOK:** *No cooking*

INGREDIENTS

½ cucumber, halved
15 g/½ oz rocket
3 fresh mint sprigs
1 courgette
1 celery stick, halved
1 apple, halved
crushed ice (optional)
1 fresh mint sprig, to garnish

1. Feed the cucumber, rocket and mint sprigs through a juicer, followed by the courgette, celery and apple halves.

2. Add a handful of crushed ice, if using, to a glass, then pour the juice over the ice.

3. Serve the juice immediately, garnished with a mint sprig.

MELON, PEAR & GINGER SPRITZER

SERVES: *1* | **PREP:** *15–20 mins* | **COOK:** *No cooking*

INGREDIENTS

½ honeydew melon, thickly sliced and peeled
1-cm/½-inch piece fresh ginger, peeled
1 pear, halved
crushed ice (optional)
125 ml/4 fl oz chilled sparkling mineral water

1. Feed the melon slices through a juicer, followed by the ginger and the pear halves.

2. Put a small handful of crushed ice, if using, into a glass, then pour the juice over the ice.

3. Top up the glass with the chilled sparkling mineral water to make a spritzer and serve immediately.

MIXED FRUIT SMOOTHIE BOWL

SERVES: *4* | **PREP:** *20 mins, plus 20 mins chilling* | **COOK:** *No cooking*

INGREDIENTS

2 papayas, peeled, deseeded and chopped
300 g/10½ oz strawberries, hulled
1 honeydew melon, peeled, deseeded and chopped
small handful of fresh mint leaves
1 tbsp stem ginger syrup
1 knob stem ginger
100 g/3½ oz blueberries
ice cubes

1. Reserving 1 tablespoon of the chopped papaya, place the remainder in a food processor with 280 g/10 oz of the strawberries and process to a smooth purée. Pour the purée into a jug and chill in the refrigerator for 10 minutes.

2. Place all but 1 tablespoon of the chopped melon in the food processor with half the mint leaves, the ginger syrup and stem ginger. Process to a smooth purée. Pour into a jug and chill in the refrigerator for 10 minutes.

3. When you are ready to serve, divide each smoothie between four bowls, then use a knife to swirl them together. Drop a couple of ice cubes into each bowl.

4. Dice the reserved fruits and sprinkle over the smoothie, together with the blueberries and the remaining mint leaves.

1
1
2

TANTALIZING TOMATO REFRESHER

SERVES: *1* | **PREP:** *10–15 mins* | **COOK:** *No cooking*

INGREDIENTS

2 carrots, halved
small handful of fresh basil leaves
1 celery stick, halved
2.5-cm/1-inch slice of broccoli stem
4 tomatoes
crushed ice (optional)

1. Feed the carrot halves through a juicer, followed by most of the basil leaves, the celery, broccoli stem slice and the tomatoes.

2. Put a small handful of crushed ice, if using, into a glass, then pour the juice over the ice.

3. Garnish with the remaining basil leaves and serve immediately.

FLU SHOT

SERVES: *1* | **PREP:** *10–15 mins* | **COOK:** *No cooking*

INGREDIENTS

½ green apple, peeled, cored and sliced
5 g/⅛ oz fresh parsley, plus a small sprig to garnish
50 g/1¾ oz cucumber
pinch of cayenne pepper
3½ tbsp chilled water

1. Put the apple slices, parsley, cucumber and cayenne pepper into a blender.

2. Add the chilled water and blend until smooth.

3. Pour the juice into a glass and serve immediately, garnished with a parsley sprig.

CHERRY AID

SERVES: *1* | **PREP:** *20 mins* | **COOK:** *No cooking*

INGREDIENTS

2 pears, halved
1 tbsp chia seeds
175 g/6 oz cherries, stoned
125 ml/4 fl oz chilled water
crushed ice (optional)

1. Feed the pear halves through a juicer.

2. Put the chia seeds in a blender and whizz until finely ground. Add the pear juice, cherries, chilled water and a handful of crushed ice, if using, and blend until smooth.

3. Pour the juice into a glass and serve immediately.

ORANGE REFRESHER

SERVES: *1* | **PREP:** *10–15 mins* | **COOK:** *No cooking*

INGREDIENTS

1 orange, zest and a little pith removed, halved
1 large fresh mint sprig
200 g/7 oz cantaloupe melon, peeled and roughly chopped
1–2 fresh mint sprigs, to decorate

1. Put the orange halves into a food processor or blender with the mint sprig and the chopped melon and process until smooth.

2. Pour the juice into a glass, and serve immediately, decorated with mint sprigs.

CELERY & APPLE REVITALIZER

SERVES: *2* | **PREP:** *10–15 mins* | **COOK:** *No cooking*

INGREDIENTS

115 g/4 oz celery, chopped
1 apple, peeled, cored and diced
600 ml/1 pint milk
pinch of sugar
salt (optional)
4 strips of celery, to garnish

1. Place the chopped celery, diced apple and milk in a blender and blend until thoroughly combined.

2. Add a pinch of sugar and a little salt, if using, and stir to combine.

3. Pour the juice into two chilled glasses, decorate with strips of celery and serve immediately.

KIWI JUICE

SERVES: *1* | **PREP:** *10 mins* | **COOK:** *No cooking*

INGREDIENTS

1 kiwi fruit, peeled and roughly chopped
1 apple, halved
115 g/4 oz seedless green grapes
crushed ice, to serve (optional)

1. Put the chopped kiwi fruit and the apple halves into a blender and blend until smooth.

2. Add the grapes and blend again until smooth and combined.

3. Put a small handful of crushed ice, if using, into a glass, pour the juice over the ice and serve immediately.

DARK BEET THIRST-QUENCHER

SERVES: *1* | **PREP:** *10–15 mins* | **COOK:** *No cooking*

INGREDIENTS

1 orange, deseeded and zest and a little pith removed
85 g/3 oz cooked beetroot
3 tbsp natural yogurt
75 ml/2½ fl oz chilled water

1. Remove a segment from the orange, cut it in half and reserve, then roughly chop the remainder.

2. Put the beetroot and orange in a blender and blend until smooth. Add the yogurt and chilled water and blend again until combined.

3. Pour the juice into a glass. Thread the reserved orange pieces through a cocktail stick, place this across the top of the glass and serve immediately.

LETTUCE ELIXIR

SERVES: *1* | **PREP:** *10–15 mins* | **COOK:** *No cooking*

INGREDIENTS

100 g/3½ oz cos lettuce, roughly chopped
4 celery sticks, roughly chopped
1 green apple, halved
25 g/1 oz fresh flat-leaf parsley
1 tsp spirulina powder
1 cos lettuce leaf, to garnish
crushed ice, to serve

1. Feed the chopped lettuce, celery and apple halves through a juicer with the parsley.

2. Stir the spirulina powder through the juice until combined.

3. Put a small handful of crushed ice, if using, into a glass, pour the juice over the ice, garnish with a lettuce leaf and serve immediately.

CITRUS CLEANSER

SERVES: *1* | **PREP:** *15 mins* | **COOK:** *No cooking*

INGREDIENTS

1 pink or ruby grapefruit, zest and a little pith removed, halved
1 orange, zest and a little pith removed, halved
1 lime, zest and pith removed, halved
1 large pear, halved
crushed ice (optional)

1. Feed the grapefruit halves, orange halves and lime halves through a juicer, followed by the pear halves.

2. Put a small handful of crushed ice, if using, into a glass.

3. Pour the juice over the ice and serve immediately.

PEACHY WAKE-UP CALL

SERVES: *1* | **PREP:** *10–15 mins* | **COOK:** *No cooking*

INGREDIENTS

1 sweet potato, cut into quarters
1-cm/½-inch piece fresh ginger
3 carrots, halved
3 peaches, halved and stoned
crushed ice (optional)
pinch of mixed spice, to serve (optional)

1. Feed the sweet potato quarters and the ginger through a juicer, followed by the carrot halves and the peach halves.

2. Put a small handful of crushed ice, if using, into a glass, then pour the juice over the ice.

3. Sprinkle the juice with a pinch of mixed spice, if using, and serve immediately.

PINK ZINGER

SERVES: *1* | **PREP:** *10–15 mins* | **COOK:** *No cooking*

INGREDIENTS

1 pink grapefruit, zest and a little pith removed, deseeded and roughly chopped
1 orange, zest and a little pith removed, deseeded and roughly chopped
½ lemon, zest and a little pith removed, deseeded and roughly chopped
½ lime, zest and a little pith removed, deseeded and roughly chopped
1–2 lime slices, to decorate

1. Place the chopped grapefruit, orange, lemon and lime in a blender and process until smooth.

2. Pour the citrus juice into a tall glass, decorate with the lime slices and serve immediately.

GREEN ENVY

SERVES: *1* | **PREP:** *10–15 mins* | **COOK:** *No cooking*

INGREDIENTS

1 green apple, cored and roughly chopped
4 celery sticks, roughly chopped
150 g/5½ oz cucumber, roughly chopped
100 g/3½ oz fresh spinach
20 g/¾ oz fresh mint leaves
1 tsp chlorophyll powder
ice cubes, to serve (optional)
1 trimmed celery stick, to garnish

1. Put the chopped apple, celery and cucumber through a juicer followed by the spinach and mint.

2. Add the chlorophyll powder to the juice and stir through until thoroughly combined.

3. Fill a glass with ice cubes, pour the juice over the ice and serve immediately, garnished with a trimmed celery stick.

FRESH COCONUT JUICE

SERVES: *2* | **PREP:** *10–15 mins* | **COOK:** *No cooking*

INGREDIENTS

2 apples, cored and cut into quarters
1 celery stick, trimmed
9-cm/3½-inch piece cucumber, quartered lengthways
200 ml/7 fl oz coconut water
celery fronds, to garnish

1. Put the apple quarters, celery stick and cucumber quarters in a food processor or blender and process until smooth.

2. Pour the juice into a jug, then add the coconut water and stir until well combined.

3. Pour the juice into two glasses, garnish with celery fronds and serve immediately.

CHAPTER FOUR

GLOW

KIWI QUENCHER

SERVES: *1* | **PREP:** *15 mins* | **COOK:** *No cooking*

INGREDIENTS

½ head of cos lettuce
4 kiwi fruit, peeled
115 g/4 oz green grapes
1 large pear, halved
crushed ice, to serve (optional)

1. Peel a leaf off the lettuce and reserve to garnish.

2. Feed the kiwi fruit and grapes through a juicer, followed by the lettuce and the pear halves.

3. Put a small handful of crushed ice, if using, into a glass, then pour the juice over the ice. Garnish with the reserved lettuce leaf and serve immediately.

BEET IT!

SERVES: *1* | **PREP:** *10–15 mins* | **COOK:** *No cooking*

INGREDIENTS

40 g/1½ oz rocket
150 g/5½ oz radicchio
40 g/1½ oz beetroot leaves
1 green apple, halved
1 beetroot, halved

1. Feed the rocket, radicchio, beetroot leaves, apple halves and beetroot halves through a juicer.

2. Stir the juice well, pour into a glass and serve immediately.

GREEN & MEAN

SERVES: *1* | **PREP:** *10 mins* | **COOK:** *No cooking*

INGREDIENTS

200 g/7 oz green grapes
20 g/¾ oz fresh flat-leaf parsley
2 carrots, roughly chopped
80 g/2 ¾ oz cavolo nero, roughly chopped
25 g/1 oz turnip leaves

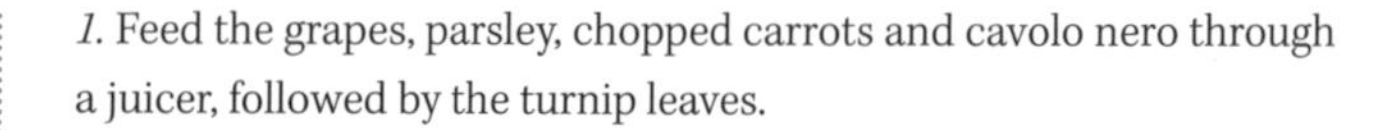

1. Feed the grapes, parsley, chopped carrots and cavolo nero through a juicer, followed by the turnip leaves.

2. Stir the juice well to combine the ingredients, pour into a glass and serve immediately.

MINTED MELON DRINK

SERVES: *1* | **PREP:** *15 mins* | **COOK:** *No cooking*

INGREDIENTS

½ honeydew melon, thickly sliced and peeled
5 fresh mint sprigs
½ lime, zest and a little pith removed
2.5-cm/1-inch slice of broccoli stem
crushed ice (optional)

1. Feed the melon slices and mint sprigs through a juicer, followed by the lime and the broccoli stem slice.

2. Put a small handful of crushed ice, if using, into a glass.

3. Pour the juice over the ice and serve immediately.

SUPER-POWERED MANGO

SERVES: *1* | **PREP:** *15–20 mins* | **COOK:** *No cooking*

INGREDIENTS

2 clementines, zest and a little pith removed
1 mango, stoned and peeled
2 apples, halved
crushed ice (optional)
chilled water, to taste
1 tsp clear honey

1. Feed the clementines, mango and apple halves through a juicer.

2. Put a small handful of crushed ice, if using, into a glass. and pour the juice over the ice.

3. Top up the glass with chilled water to taste, stir in the honey and serve immediately.

AÇAI FROZEN SMOOTHIE BOWL

SERVES: *4* | **PREP:** *10–15 mins, plus 2 hours freezing* | **COOK:** *8–10 mins*

INGREDIENTS

2 bananas, peeled and sliced
300 g/10½ oz raspberries
100 g/3½ oz rolled oats
2 tbsp dried cranberries
1 tbsp sunflower seeds
3 tbsp maple syrup
100 ml/3½ fl oz non-dairy milk
1 tbsp açai powder
100 g/3½ oz blueberries

1. Arrange the banana slices and 200 g/7 oz of the raspberries in a single layer on a tray and freeze for at least 2 hours.

2. Preheat a grill to medium-hot. Mix the oats, cranberries, sunflower seeds and maple syrup together and spread over a baking sheet.

3. Cook under the preheated grill for 8–10 minutes, turning frequently, until golden (watch them carefully as they can suddenly burn). Leave to cool.

4. Meanwhile, place half the frozen banana in a food processor with half the frozen raspberries and half the milk. Process until broken down. With the machine running slowly add the açai powder and the remaining banana, raspberries and milk, adding enough milk to produce an ice cream consistency.

5. Divide between four bowls, top with the blueberries and sprinkle with the maple-toasted oats.

1
2
4

UP THE ANTI

SERVES: *1* | **PREP:** *15–20 mins, plus chilling* | **COOK:** *No cooking*

INGREDIENTS

½ avocado, stoned, flesh scooped from the skin and chopped
115 g/4 oz blueberries
115 g/4 oz strawberries, hulled
juice of 1 tangerine or small orange
125 ml/4 fl oz chilled water
crushed ice (optional)

1. Put the chopped avocado, the blueberries, strawberries, tangerine juice and chilled water into a blender and whizz to combine.

2. Add a small handful of crushed ice, if using, and whizz again until smooth and combined.

3. Pour into a tall glass and serve immediately.

GREEN COLADA

SERVES: *1* | **PREP:** *10–15 mins* | **COOK:** *No cooking*

INGREDIENTS

100 g/3½ oz spinach, roughly chopped
100 g/3½ oz cucumber, roughly chopped
20 g/¾ oz fresh mint leaves
200 ml/7 fl oz coconut milk
½ tsp linseeds
1 tsp chlorophyll powder
1 fresh mint sprig, to garnish
crushed ice, to serve

1. Feed the chopped spinach and cucumber through a juicer, followed by the mint leaves.

2. Add the coconut milk, linseeds and chlorophyll powder and stir through the juice until thoroughly combined.

3. Fill a glass with crushed ice, pour the juice over the ice, garnish with a mint sprig and serve immediately.

BLACKBERRY BLASTER

SERVES: *1* | **PREP:** *15 mins* | **COOK:** *No cooking*

INGREDIENTS

3 large red-skinned plums, halved and stoned
40 g/1½ oz red curly kale
1 pear, halved
115 g/4 oz blackberries
20 g/¾ oz wheat germ
¼ tsp ground cinnamon (optional)
crushed ice
4–6 tbsp chilled water

1. Feed the plum halves, then the kale, then the pear halves through a juicer. Pour the juice into a blender.

2. Add the blackberries (reserving one to decorate), wheat germ, cinnamon, if using, and a small handful of crushed ice and blend until smooth and combined.

3. Add chilled water to taste and blend again until smooth. Pour the juice into a glass.

4. Thread the reserved blackberry onto a cocktail stick and use this to decorate the glass, then serve immediately.

PEAR, BEETROOT & SPINACH JUICE

SERVES: *1* | **PREP:** *10–15 mins* | **COOK:** *No cooking*

INGREDIENTS

1 beetroot, trimmed, peeled and chopped
1 pear, cored and chopped
25 g/1 oz fresh spinach leaves
filtered water, to taste
1 spinach leaf, to decorate

1. Place the chopped beetroot, chopped pear and spinach in a food processor or blender and process until smooth.

2. Dilute the juice with a little filtered water to taste.

3. Pour the juice into a cocktail glass, decorate with the spinach leaf and serve immediately.

GREEN APPLE & KIWI JUICE

SERVES: *2* | **PREP:** *10–15 mins* | **COOK:** *No cooking*

INGREDIENTS

2 green apples, such as Granny Smith, halved
½ cucumber, roughly chopped
2 kiwi fruit, peeled and roughly chopped
½ lemon, zest and pith removed, deseeded and roughly chopped
2-cm/¾-inch piece fresh ginger, peeled and roughly chopped

1. Feed the apple halves, chopped cucumber, kiwi fruit, lemon and ginger through a juicer.

2. Pour the juice into two tall glasses and serve immediately.

WHEATGRASS JUICE CLEANSER

SERVES: *2* | **PREP:** *15 mins* | **COOK:** *No cooking*

INGREDIENTS

3–4 carrots,, roughly chopped
1 beetroot, roughly chopped
4 celery sticks, roughly chopped
1 cucumber, roughly chopped
½ lemon
small handful of fresh parsley or mint
50 ml/2 fl oz wheatgrass juice
chilled water, to taste
2 celery sticks, to serve

1. Feed the chopped carrots, beetroot, celery and cucumber through a juicer.

2. Feed the lemon and parsley through the juicer. Add the wheatgrass juice and chilled water to taste and stir well to combine.

3. Pour the juice into two glasses and serve immediately with the celery sticks.

SPROUT TONIC

SERVES: *1* | **PREP:** *10–15 mins* | **COOK:** *No cooking*

INGREDIENTS

75 g/2¾ oz Brussels sprouts
25 g/1 oz beetroot leaves
25 g/1 oz chard
250 ml/9 fl oz unsweetened rice milk

1. Put the Brussels sprouts, beetroot leaves and chard into a blender.

2. Pour over the rice milk and blend until smooth and creamy.

3. Pour the smoothie into a glass and serve immediately.

RUBY FRUIT REVIVER

SERVES: *1* | **PREP:** *15–20 mins* | **COOK:** *No cooking*

INGREDIENTS

1 ruby red grapefruit, zest and a little pith removed, deseeded and roughly chopped
¼ cucumber, roughly chopped
150 g/5½ oz strawberries, hulled
crushed ice (optional)

1. Put the chopped grapefruit and cucumber into a blender and whizz until smooth.

2. Add the strawberries and a handful of crushed ice, if using, and whizz again until smooth and combined.

3. Pour the juice into a glass and serve immediately.

1

2

3

MIXED BERRY SMOOTHIE

SERVES: *4* | **PREP:** *10 mins* | **COOK:** *No cooking*

INGREDIENTS

1 tbsp chia seeds (preferably white)
375 ml/13 fl oz soya milk
125 g/4½ oz frozen mixed berries, slightly thawed
1 ripe banana, peeled and sliced
3 ready-to-eat dried apricots, roughly chopped
2 tbsp honey
2 tsp lemon juice
4 tsp frozen mixed berries, slightly thawed, to decorate

1. Put the chia seeds into a small bowl. Stir in 125 ml/4 fl oz of the soya milk and leave to soak for 15 minutes, whisking every 5 minutes to prevent the seeds clumping together.

2. Put the mixed berries, banana slices, chopped apricots, honey and lemon juice into a blender. Add the soaked chia seeds with their gel-like liquid.

3. Whizz for 1 minute or until smooth. Pour the smoothie into four glasses, decorate with a few berries and serve immediately.

DANDELION COOLER

SERVES: *1* | **PREP:** *10–15 mins* | **COOK:** *No cooking*

INGREDIENTS

25 g/1 oz dandelion leaves
25 g/1 oz watercress
200 ml/7 fl oz chilled water
1 large pear, deseeded and chopped
3½ tbsp coconut cream
ice cubes, to serve

1. Put the dandelion leaves, watercress and chilled water into a blender and blend until smooth.

2. Add the chopped pear to the blender with the coconut cream, then blend again until smooth and creamy.

3. Put some ice cubes into a glass, then stir the juice well, pour it over the ice and serve immediately.

FRESH & FRUITY

SERVES: *1* | **PREP:** *10–15 mins* | **COOK:** *No cooking*

INGREDIENTS

½ small pineapple, peeled and roughly chopped
85 g/3 oz blackberries
85 g/3 oz blueberries
1 tsp goji berries, roughly chopped, to decorate

1. Put the chopped pineapple into a blender with the blackberries and blueberries and blend until smooth.

2. Pour the juice into a glass, sprinkle with the chopped goji berries and serve immediately.

CRANBERRY SOOTHER

SERVES: *1* | **PREP:** *10 mins* | **COOK:** *No cooking*

INGREDIENTS

150 g/5½ oz cranberries
juice of 1 orange
5 tbsp natural yogurt
2 tsp clear honey

1. Put the cranberries and orange juice into a blender or food processor and blend until smooth.

2. Add the yogurt and honey and blend again until the mixture is smooth and combined.

3. Pour the smoothie into a glass and serve immediately.

CHERRY PINK

SERVES: *1* | **PREP:** *20–25 mins* | **COOK:** *No cooking*

INGREDIENTS

350 g/12 oz dark sweet cherries, stoned
1 apple, halved
½ lime, zest and pith removed, deseeded and roughly chopped
100 g/3½ oz red grapes
40 g/1½ oz soya yogurt

1. Put the cherries, apple halves, chopped lime and grapes into a blender and blend until smooth.

2. Whisk in the yogurt, then pour the juice into a glass and serve.

GRAPE NUTRIENT-BOOSTER

SERVES: *1* | **PREP:** *15 mins* | **COOK:** *No cooking*

INGREDIENTS

2 pears, halved
¼ small head of Savoy cabbage, roughly chopped
1 tbsp pumpkin seeds
150 g/5½ oz seedless green grapes
small handful of crushed ice (optional)

1. Feed the pear halves and chopped cabbage through a juicer.

2. Put the pumpkin seeds into a blender and whizz until finely ground, then add the grapes and a handful of crushed ice, if using, and blend.

3. Add the pear juice mix to the blender and blend until smooth. Pour the juice into a glass and serve immediately.

MANGO & LIME BONE-BUILDER

SERVES: *1* | **PREP:** *15 mins* | **COOK:** *No cooking*

INGREDIENTS

1 tbsp sesame seeds
juice of ½ lime
25 g/1 oz green curly kale, shredded
1 mango, peeled, stoned and roughly chopped
225 ml/8 fl oz unsweetened rice, almond or soya milk
crushed ice

1. Put the sesame seeds into a blender and whizz until finely ground.

2. Add the lime juice, shredded kale and chopped mango and blend until well combined.

3. Add the rice milk and a small handful of crushed ice and blend again until smooth. Pour into a glass and serve immediately.

CHAPTER FIVE

SOOTHE

PLUM POWER

SERVES: *1* | **PREP:** *10–15 mins* | **COOK:** *20 mins, plus cooling*

INGREDIENTS

125 g/4½ oz plums, stoned
100 ml/3½ fl oz water
2 tsp clear honey
2 scoops natural frozen yogurt
1 Italian almond or pistachio biscotti, crumbled, to decorate (optional)
¼ plum, stoned, to decorate (optional)

1. Put the plums, water and honey into a small saucepan over a medium heat. Stir, cover tightly, then reduce the heat to low and simmer for 15 minutes until the plums have split and are very soft. Leave to cool.

2. Pour the mixture into a blender, then add the frozen yogurt and blend until smooth.

3. Pour the smoothie into a glass, sprinkle over the crumbled biscotti, if using, decorate the rim of the glass with the plum quarter, if using, and serve immediately.

CUCUMBER SOOTHER

SERVES: *1* | **PREP:** *10–15 mins* | **COOK:** *No cooking*

INGREDIENTS

1 large pear, halved
100 g/3½ oz cucumber, roughly chopped
1 green apple, halved
10 g/¼ oz fresh mint leaves
1 tbsp aloe vera gel
crushed ice, to serve (optional)
1 cucumber slice, to garnish
1 fresh mint sprig, to garnish

1. Feed the pear halves, chopped cucumber and apple halves through a juicer with the mint leaves.

2. Add the aloe vera gel to the juice and stir through until combined. Put a handful of crushed ice, if using, into a glass, then pour the juice over the ice.

3. Serve the juice immediately, garnished with a cucumber slice and a mint sprig.

BERRY WHIP

SERVES: *4* | **PREP:** *10–15 mins* | **COOK:** *No cooking*

INGREDIENTS

125 g/4½ oz frozen sliced strawberries
125 g/4½ oz frozen blueberries
40 g/1½ oz Brazil nuts
40 g/1½ oz cashew nut pieces
25 g/1 oz porridge oats
450 ml/16 fl oz almond milk
2 tbsp maple syrup

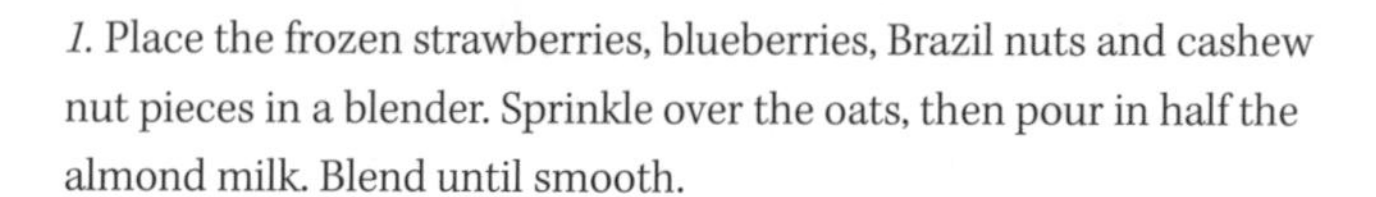

1. Place the frozen strawberries, blueberries, Brazil nuts and cashew nut pieces in a blender. Sprinkle over the oats, then pour in half the almond milk. Blend until smooth.

2. Add the remaining almond milk and the maple syrup and blend until smooth and combined.

3. Pour the smoothie into four glasses and serve immediately with spoons. As the drink stands, the blueberries will almost set the liquid, but as soon as you stir it, it will turn to liquid again.

VANILLA, ALMOND & BANANA SMOOTHIE

SERVES: *2* | **PREP:** *5 mins* | **COOK:** *No cooking*

INGREDIENTS

225 ml/8 fl oz almond milk
60 g/2¼ oz almond butter
1 banana, peeled and roughly chopped
4 stoned dates
1 tsp vanilla extract
8–10 ice cubes

1. Place the almond milk, almond butter, chopped banana, dates and vanilla extract in a blender.

2. Add the ice cubes and blend until smooth and combined.

3. Pour the smoothie into two tall glasses and serve immediately with straws.

GO NUTS

SERVES: *1* | **PREP:** *10–15 mins* | **COOK:** *No cooking*

INGREDIENTS

½ avocado, stoned, flesh scooped from the skin and chopped
4 Brazil nuts
3 Medjool dates
10 g/¼ oz fresh ginger, peeled
350 ml/12 fl oz almond milk
¼ tsp ground cinnamon
crushed ice, to serve (optional)

1. Place the chopped avocado, nuts, dates and ginger in a blender and blend until smooth and creamy.

2. Pour over the almond milk, add the cinnamon and blend again until smooth and combined.

3. Put a small handful of crushed ice, if using, into a glass, then pour the smoothie over the ice and serve immediately.

PINEAPPLE PUMP

SERVES: *1* | **PREP:** *10–15 mins* | **COOK:** *No cooking*

INGREDIENTS

5 celery sticks, roughly chopped
150 g/5½ oz curly green kale, shredded
150 g/5½ oz fresh pineapple, peeled, cored and roughly chopped
25 g/1 oz fresh mint leaves
1 tsp wheatgrass powder
1 small slice of fresh pineapple, to garnish
1 kale leaf, to garnish

1. Feed the chopped celery, shredded kale and chopped pineapple through a juicer with the mint leaves.

2. Add the wheatgrass powder to the juice and stir well to combine.

3. Pour the juice into a glass and serve immediately, garnished with the slice of pineapple and a kale leaf.

GRAPE & LYCHEE REVIVER

SERVES: *1* | **PREP:** *15 mins* | **COOK:** *No cooking*

INGREDIENTS

300 g/10½ oz green grapes
55 g/2 oz young spinach
½ ripe avocado, stoned, flesh scooped from the skin and chopped
5 lychees, peeled and stoned
crushed ice
125 ml/4 fl oz chilled water
1 avocado slice, to serve (optional)

1. Feed the grapes and spinach through a juicer.

2. Pour the juice into a blender, add the chopped avocado, lychees and a small handful of crushed ice and blend until smooth.

3. Add the chilled water and blend again. Pour the juice into a glass, add the avocado slice, if using, and serve immediately.

BERRY POWER

SERVES: *1* | **PREP:** *15 mins* | **COOK:** *No cooking*

INGREDIENTS

20 g/¾ oz pumpkin seeds
20 g/¾ oz linseeds
20 g/¾ oz flaked almonds
115 g/4 oz raspberries
115 g/4 oz blueberries
225 g/8 oz vanilla soya yogurt
125 ml/4 fl oz chilled water

1. Put the pumpkin seeds, linseeds and almonds into a blender and whizz until finely ground.

2. Add the raspberries, blueberries, yogurt and chilled water to the blender and blend until smooth and combined.

3. Pour the smoothie into a glass and serve immediately.

SUPER SMOOTHIE

SERVES: *1* | **PREP:** *10–15 mins* | **COOK:** *No cooking*

INGREDIENTS

25 g/1 oz spinach leaves
250 ml/9 fl oz cooled liquorice tea
½ avocado, stoned, flesh scooped from the skin and chopped
1 frozen banana
1 tsp chia seeds
½ tsp chia seeds, to garnish

1. Put the spinach leaves and liquorice tea into a blender and blend until smooth.

2. Add the chopped avocado to the blender with the banana and chia seeds and blend until smooth and creamy.

3. Pour the smoothie into a glass, garnish with a sprinkling of chia seeds and serve immediately with a straw.

BEAT THE MORNING BLUES

SERVES: *1* | **PREP:** *10–15 mins* | **COOK:** *No cooking*

INGREDIENTS

1 pear, halved
150 g/5½ oz blueberries
100 g/3½ oz soya yogurt
½ tsp agave syrup
2 tsp flaked almonds, toasted

1. Feed the pear halves through a juicer. Pour the juice into a blender, then add the blueberries and blend until smooth.

2. Add the yogurt and agave syrup to the blender and blend again until smooth and combined.

3. Pour the smoothie into a glass, sprinkle with the flaked almonds and serve immediately.

GUAVA SMOOTHIE

SERVES: *2* | **PREP:** *10 mins* | **COOK:** *No cooking*

INGREDIENTS

400 g/14 oz canned guavas, drained
225 ml/8 fl oz milk

1. Place the guavas in a food processor or blender and pour the milk over them.

2. Process the guavas and milk until smooth and combined.

3. Strain the smoothie into two glasses to remove the hard guava seeds, then serve immediately.

MORNING POWERBOWL SMOOTHIE

SERVES: *1* | **PREP:** *10 mins* | **COOK:** *No cooking*

INGREDIENTS

50 g/1¾ oz strawberries
50 g/1¾ oz blackberries
50 g/1¾ oz raspberries
1 banana, peeled and halved
150 ml/5 fl oz hemp milk
1 tbsp coconut oil
1 tbsp ground almonds
1 kiwi fruit, peeled and sliced
2 tsp chia seeds
1 small mango, peeled, stoned and chopped
1 tbsp chopped walnuts
2 tsp toasted sesame seeds

1. Place the strawberries, blackberries, raspberries and half the banana in a blender.

2. Add the hemp milk, coconut oil and ground almonds and blend until smooth and combined.

3. Slice the remaining half banana. Pour the smoothie into a bowl, arrange the banana slices, kiwi fruit slices, chia seeds, chopped mango, chopped walnuts and sesame seeds decoratively on top and serve immediately.

MELON & COCONUT MOJITO

SERVES: *1* | **PREP:** *10–15 mins* | **COOK:** *No cooking*

INGREDIENTS

20 g/¾ oz spinach leaves
50 g/1¾ oz coconut flesh
200 ml/7 fl oz chilled water
100 g/3½ oz cantaloupe melon, peeled, deseeded and chopped
1 tbsp chopped fresh mint
juice of ½ lime
50 g/1¾ oz mango, stoned and peeled
1 mango slice, to garnish
crushed ice, to serve

1. Put the spinach leaves, coconut flesh and chilled water into a blender and blend until smooth (this might take a little longer than usual as the coconut flesh is quite dense).

2. Add the chopped melon, mint, lime juice and mango and blend again until smooth and creamy.

3. Put a small handful of crushed ice, if using, into a glass, garnish with the mango slice and serve immediately with a straw.

BROCCOLI BOOSTER

SERVES: *1* | **PREP:** *10–15 mins* | **COOK:** *No cooking*

INGREDIENTS

150 g/5½ oz broccoli stem, roughly chopped
75 g/2¾ oz spinach leaves
200 ml/7 fl oz chilled water
1 frozen banana
1 tbsp pumpkin seed butter
1 tbsp manuka honey

1. Put the chopped broccoli stem in a blender with the spinach leaves and chilled water and blend until smooth.

2. Add the banana, pumpkin seed butter and honey and blend again until smooth and creamy.

3. Pour the smoothie into a glass and serve immediately with a straw.

STOMACH SOOTHER

SERVES: *1* | **PREP:** *15 mins* | **COOK:** *No cooking*

INGREDIENTS

½ sweet pineapple, peeled and cut into thick slices
1 lemon, zest and most of the pith removed, halved
2-cm/¾-inch piece fresh ginger, peeled
1 pineapple leaf, to decorate (optional)

1. Feed the pineapple slices and the lemon halves through a juicer with the ginger.

2. Pour the juice into a glass, add the pineapple leaf as a stirrer, if using, and serve immediately. (Remove the pineapple leaf before drinking as it's very sharp.)

1
1
2

CHOCOLATE BANANA SMOOTHIE

SERVES: *1* | **PREP:** *10–15 mins* | **COOK:** *No cooking*

INGREDIENTS

½ banana, peeled and sliced
55 g/2 oz silken tofu, drained and roughly chopped
160 ml /5½ fl oz reduced-fat soya milk
1 tbsp clear honey
2 tbsp cocoa powder
¼ tsp vanilla extract

1. Put the banana slices, chopped tofu, soya milk, honey, cocoa powder and vanilla extract into a blender.

2. Blend on high speed until combined and smooth, making sure that the cocoa powder has been fully incorporated with the rest of the ingredients.

3. Pour the smoothie into a tall glass and serve immediately.

HAIL THE KALE

SERVES: *1* | **PREP:** *10–15 mins* | **COOK:** *No cooking*

INGREDIENTS

25 g/1 oz green curly kale, shredded
50 g/1¾ oz coconut flesh
350 ml/12 fl oz chilled almond milk
1 tbsp sunflower seeds
¼ tsp ground cinnamon
¼ tsp ground cinnamon, to garnish

1. Put the shredded kale in a blender, then add the coconut flesh, almond milk, sunflower seeds and cinnamon.

2. Blend until smooth and creamy (this might take a little longer than usual as the coconut flesh is quite dense).

3. Pour into a glass and serve immediately, sprinkled with a little ground cinnamon.

THE GRASSHOPPER

SERVES: *1* | **PREP:** *10–15 mins* | **COOK:** *No cooking*

INGREDIENTS

20 g/¾ oz courgette, chopped
1 small celery stick, chopped
10 g/½ oz watercress
juice of ½ lemon
1 tbsp chilled water
courgette slice, to garnish

1. Put the chopped courgette and celery into a blender. Add the watercress and lemon juice.

2. Pour over the chilled water and blend until smooth and combined.

3. Transfer to a glass, garnish with a small slice of courgette and serve immediately.

TURBO RECHARGER

SERVES: *1* | **PREP:** *20 mins* | **COOK:** *No cooking*

INGREDIENTS

½ honeydew melon, deseeded and roughly chopped
1 banana, peeled and roughly chopped
1 kiwi fruit, peeled and roughly chopped
115 g/4 oz seedless green grapes
small handful of watercress
125 ml/4 fl oz unsweetened rice, almond or soya milk
crushed ice (optional)

1. Put the chopped melon, banana and kiwi fruit into a blender with the grapes and watercress.

2. Blend until smooth and combined, then add the rice milk and a small handful of crushed ice, if using.

3. Blend again until combined, then pour the smoothie into a tall glass and serve immediately.

SUPER GREENS

SERVES: *1* | **PREP:** *15–15 mins* | **COOK:** *No cooking*

INGREDIENTS

1 pear, halved
40 g/1½ oz young spinach leaves
4 fresh flat-leaf parsley sprigs
¼ cucumber, roughly chopped
½ avocado, stoned, flesh scooped from the skin and chopped
½ tsp spirulina powder
chilled water, to taste
1 Brazil nut, roughly chopped

1. Feed the pear halves through a juicer then pour the juice into a blender. Add the spinach leaves, parsley sprigs, chopped cucumber and avocado and blend until smooth.

2. Mix the spirulina powder with just enough chilled water to make a thick liquid.

3. Pour the juice into a glass and swirl the spirulina mixture into the juice. Sprinkle over the chopped Brazil nut and serve immediately.

INDEX

This edition published by Parragon Books Ltd in 2017
LOVE FOOD is an imprint of Parragon Books Ltd

Parragon Books Ltd
Chartist House
15–17 Trim Street
Bath BA1 1HA, UK
www.parragon.co.uk/love-food
www.parragon.com.au/love-food

ISBN 978-1-4748-6897-6

Printed in China

Introduction by Sarah Bush
Edited by Fiona Biggs
Cover photography by Al Richardson

The cover shot shows Super-powered Mango on page 125, Blackberry Blaster on page 133 and Super Smoothie on page 170.

Notes for the Reader

This book uses both metric and imperial measurements. Follow the same units of measurement throughout; do not mix metric and imperial. All spoon measurements are level: teaspoons are assumed to be 5 ml, and tablespoons are assumed to be 15 ml. Unless otherwise stated, milk is assumed to be full fat, eggs and individual fruits and vegetables are medium, pepper is freshly ground black pepper and salt is table salt. Unless otherwise stated, all root vegetables should be peeled prior to using.

The times given are an approximate guide only. Preparation times differ according to the techniques used by different people and the cooking times may also vary from those given.